an indigo scent after
the rain

an indigo scent after the rain

poems by James Grabill

Lynx House Press
Portland, Oregon/ Spokane, Washington

Cover and Book Design by Christine Holbert
Cover Art by James Grabill

The author wishes to extend special thanks to Christopher Howell for his
collaborative assistance and insights, and to Diane Averill, Tim Barnes, John
Bradley, Gerald Fleming, George Kalamaras, Sue Mach, Michael McDowell,
Verlena Orr, Josh Otto, Paulann Petersen, Dan Raphael, Paul Roth, William
Tremblay, and William Witherup for deep-currented correspondence, talk of
craft, encouragement, and/or camaraderie.

Lynx House Press
420 W. 24th Ave.
Spokane, WA 99203
and
9305 SE Salmon Ct.
Portland, OR 97216

Library of Congress Cataloging-in-Publication Data

Grabill, James, 1949-
     An Indigo scent after the rain / James Grabill
     p. cm.
     ISBN 0-89924-113-1 (alk. paper)
     I. Title

PS3557.R115 I53 2002
                                        2002073189

Table of Contents

for Marilyn,
whose love and support is a fuel and
balancing and thriving garden

I.

It can't be the passing of time that casts

That white shadow across the waters

Just off shore.

—James Wright

Night Sky

The night sky fills each cell with a billion fires.
They must be so hot and magnificent
we cannot imagine them
except abstractly.

Because it's inside, the night sky.
It's under room light and thickness,
surrounding it all, inside it all,
the root calls and burning 1942 ship.
And that little girl sitting at a wooden table.

That is, each of her bodily cells
is swimming in the night sky.
Each molecule of each of her cells
dwells in the night sky.

Anywhere light has been radiating its spheres,
creating matter, what matters, what is seen
by consciousness, everywhere the night sky holds.
Each glass of water the night sky holds.
Each coat by the door
is made up of night sky.

Take those eighth grade boys in the locker room,
with the night sky's billions of suns
and galaxies and unseen planets
filling all consciousness. Or the sea shell
on the shelf—the night sky has it
entirely, the way a year we have abandoned

rests. If you see your mother in a room,
say, all living cells, all particles of matter,
everything is carried in the womb of night sky.

When she dies, does the wheel sweep
through all her prayers, bringing her up
into another place? Life has formed here
unthinkably, and life goes unthinkably
already full of night galaxies in the vast sky,

these fibers made up of that night.

Hieroglyphics from Wind
and the Inside of Seeds

The winds bend long grasses
over anthills and wavering
doubt in poplar branches
down here in sound
over brick streets.
All that prethinking
before anything appears—the wind
has been threading a tiniest edge,
bending us, some slow rhythm
of intersections steady,
as if all this were the life.

Human actions lift
in sparks making, say,
an ancient Greek city,
and they anchor soundly
underneath glowing iron
shadows, turbines lit up
by thought that made them
held by what is near.

The apple's birds
are more places
than we learn.

Distant highway trucks
barrel down open road.
Gravity ignites or lays low
or feels like bones in the body.
All the reaches and throws,
so much is forgotten,
like hearing a bodily chord
that vanishes in sounds
of simple breathing.

Who we are, how we love,
what is gone will linger
and, by being, soon be gone.

Berries form and storms
complete the sky.
And wild open space
of universe shows the ant
and rose where to cross
in blossoming air. Moon
scooping out part of the ocean
lets the city suffer, and sleep,
and exalt in its atoms and cradles.

**

A huge carved door holds back the English stories.
A cream-colored horse ridden by the wind
of its actual birth is multiplied by the sun.
Beach fires fill a ring. Conjoined absences
conceive. Present spinach shows up
from its other life in a Tibetan mandala,
a tiny touch of it. For the spiraling, saucering
galaxy loosens seeds into flying native geese
inside magnetic rethinking, the sweltering
tip of a frond that is an entire business,
a whole country pulled taut by a spider.

The stones pouring
out of a shovel, heat
swelling from brain-lit cells,
old desire is our asking.
Forgive us when we've been
wrong. Cool air in the dawn
of this next place can heal
a system round. Some
seeds know how to give
their strength to a world.
Some know how to make
the sun a food.

A struck gong already dissolved used to be
doctrine, used to be long boats, used to be
no-doctrine, contracting and expanding,
contracting and laying out cities, attracting
the young, the ocean wave crashing,
the night sky inhaling much of the endless world.

This Light, This Lightning

Imagine a person we know, taken
back by the wind. Imagine her
now rain in the place
where she is not present.

The flashing crack of lightning
seeds each eggshell sentence.
The ocean silently rises, engulfing
whatever has been left, those tiny candles
on the beach where we were.

My father, anyone's father,
I cannot imagine him being
swept out into waves forever.
Is that all, leaving the planet,
leaving personage, becoming
nothing at all, nothing at all,
nothing at all, man,
nothing at all?

The wide circlings starcharts show
that plants responded to
rotating their leaves as their genes
turned, listening, rooting in,
are the thumbprints of all vanishing.

A rhino in Africa suddenly
is no more. A mother
in lightning flash is taken
back by the lightning

that brought breathing to this place,
that kindled thinking
from inside its rock.

This evening, we live, we are blessed
by this place and this light
the ocean of night sky carries.
I look at the candle
and see a year far away
breathing through us as we breathe.

This light, it gives us a grant
of everything we can think of.

Walking as the Air Cools Slightly

Tonight we walked under streetlamps
by neighboring houses in half-light
and felt close in, on some kind of path.
We walked through the neighborhood
and found a hill where we looked west,
almost able to see light reflect
off the ocean.
                        We walked through the feel
of evening cedar scent, cut grasses,
moist coolness from soil after one
of the heated-up days, in a time
when scientists measure light, computing
125 billion or so galaxies swim the universe
as brilliant nautiluses, spiraling motion in gravity,
the collie running beside us a while,
a few blossoming trees lingering
a scent from wild places, in this time
of immense outer space telescopes
recording light fourteen billion
years old. And what have we been asking it?
Is it inhabited itself as it reaches us,
steadily, the speed it has always known
to go? Or is that just how we know it?
Consider a light year
                        is 5.88 trillion
miles of travel, and the nearest sun to ours
has been understood 4.3 light years away.
If this star, Alpha Centauri, has a planet
with life, how long would it take personnel
to show up there in a massive Earth fleet?

Anyway, that place is more than one star
and probably without planets, with two
of its three stars orbiting each other
every 80 years, though we give them one name.
Maybe beings there are somehow embodied fire,
but what would we ask? How could we tell?

Tonight we walked in the evening, after one
of the spring days, and felt close in,
under streetlamps, on some kind of path
we sense from ways we've been waking,
where the psyche is grown by its story,
where ancestors' drums still reach the body.

Was It Like Drinking Water
Out of the Rain?

After working for flat money, working for clear position,
   what can you say to the girl who looks bored?
After working for the blue, for the light,
   for the silk string of the spider,
   what can you say to the loan officer?
After syntaxing primordial parentage,
   ticketing red-gray smoldering, what tone
   of voice is best for making the least order?
After heaving up the end of a fallen branch,
   leaving an iridescent beetle in his gorge,
   what do you say to a mountain? To the moss?

How is it a punch press smacks through the flat steel
   every thirty seconds though we didn't vote on the mold?
Who is that long man lifting his yellow-white apple hat
   and stretching his august lips back through memory?
Are the old brick apartment houses still full of thought
   and do they still sit on those grandmother basements?
Do the jets still boom through the 50s in forward progress
   when someone in the world needs to be held?

Say people fail and succeed, meaning and nonmeaning
   grow like ferns, a boy is water
   drunk out of the rain—where
   do you plant the trophy of sadness?
Say someone imagined herself one of them,
   say someone tried to be just a naked human
   in his body—could you call
   when it is evening?

Say all the while he worked like a road,
  say she was alert in a country you never were,
  after working for ancestors then knowing not to,
  after living certain roots of what will come—
  can you feel light on the wild Pacific stone
  and longings of the first-lit
  cathedral firs?

Under the Sun

One day you look around;
the next day you know where to go.

One day you're a member of the club;
the next day the country plunges through 1970.

One day you have a touring car,
the next day a dump truck of cinders.

You have a marriage or you don't one day;
you are single or you aren't the next day.

One day you think you are almost your parents;
the next day you wander like someone on shore leave.

One day you search for a place to relax;
the next day you have to save your soul.

A few aches follow you around one day;
a few days follow you for years one day.

One day you have rain in your hair,
the next day young people going to war.

One day you look for the steaming exit;
the next day you ask the right question.

One day you have the sky or a raccoon;
the next day you have a yellow car.

One day you have hair to your shoulders;
one day an old person lives in your body.

One day you know where to go,
but the next day you look around
like someone driving under the trees.

Some Adult Theater

People in the military call where they live
up to their potential a theater, maybe to emphasize
they aren't really soldiers, generals, or cooks

for the units. Likewise, when we work, do we go
to another theater, where what we aren't really
is what we are? Is all work a theater, and if so,

then why don't we all belong to the same union
of actors on the planet at this point in time?
Why don't we all have a solid benefits package?

And if this all is so, then where is it we become
the us ourselves, virtually catching up with it all?
Sometimes I have this feeling there are directors

out ahead of us, planning the weeks and months
of how things go, some like shamen wearing crow bodies,
all the molten molecules washed out into the straits,

the mathematical equations of relative weights
and movements scribbled in a physicist's notebook.
But now I want to claim this time on behalf

of the blue and light, in the name of youngsters
piercing their noses, in the wake of the wave
militaristically passing through organizational

calendars of spirit-minded administrative assistants,
in the face of oblivion that few actually consider,
in the make-up of the scent of marigolds that breathe

all summer under the riches, in the family story
slicked up with saliva so it will pass through
the eye of the needle, in the curtains thrown open

over the red plateaus and mulch piles with loss
layered into phrases, and in the look in the face
of a little girl in the new store, surrounded

by massive aisles of adult choices, in the cinnamon
and taste of parsley, in the tomato sauce and oystery
chanting, in the vibrato of singers of the formal songs,

in the mica glimmering on the path in foothills,
in the bugle of the elk for fallen timber,
in the tirade of a man on the beach of nakedness,

in the scent of a lover's hair and the bed sheets,
in the slownesses and speeds and outsmartings,
and in cactus palaces and mansions of top soil,

in the scent of tablets and sharpened pencils
guiding us back to whole numbers carefully,
back to a felt scent of the question

we come with, back to the evening marsh
of particles, flocks modifying each touch,
in the name of process, and of justice.

Three from the Oregon Coast

I. Driftwood Stump on the Beach

At Seaside, the ocean washed up an immense gray stump. Who knows when or why someone tried to burn it? They didn't get very far. Time didn't pass. The brown sand drifted, a bottle cap surfaced, and chipped-open shells held sea gulls in their wind.

The rubber-suited surfer went back out. A women in dark blue walked further and bent down. The yards moved in their miles. A woman walked and nothing much moved. In the ocean wind, the buildings had been there and had been there.

II. Coastal Groves

Ocean of firs moving inland, and so much longing that went out being pulled back in, taken into the trunk, and deeper, into ancient rock of the sun. There is the fir root dropping, falling in dream, and listened down in waking, as its body.

There is no bottom of it, the root is saying, growing, holding down. You never fall past its new growing, its only touching down for you. "It is the root of the world going down," Doug said he thought in one of the dreams.

Dream fir, walk with my body through the earth and rise with me on waking.

III. Woman Who Looks Like a Dancer

She was touching the moss, and carrying shells around her neck or in her hand, bending, moving slowly then quickly. Blue and gray-brown feathers were on her belt and on the dash in her van. The scent of the evening forest floor maintained a house we could go to, a house of the ocean forest, of the open sky.

I forget too often to fill my whole body, before returning. I forget too often to go there where she is listening and waking then my listening, where shadows from the green breathing soothe any of the dark water for a time.

Elegy

He did love her. And now the stories fall away.
Now the stone-lit fog brightens and fades.
The motor cars drift ahead and back in simple thinking.
     Tatters flag down the dream from the photography.
          All liquid stops.
        Now the sun's a crow.
     Everything must come to dust,
        as the poet wrote.

  These lives, so long, we think them through.
    Nothing turns out the same.
   The hawk flies over a far-off ranch.
The salmon rushes up into the red wave from the center
      of earth, invisible, silver
       in black current, blue in expanses and worry,
    dark red in the blood from inside earth of us.

When everything passes, will it seem lit by ocean floors?
         Will it carry itself for long?
          The feathery rent in the swirl,
      in the ocean soup we came from—
   what is it we might return to?

  The black flower of water is everything-jazz.
  The pounding machinery from inside a word like *heat*
    follows him off into that cold.
  When he has gone, it is south
    and north, yes and no.

Is it like the feel of a boat,
harbored, after solidness dissolves?

The stone walls bleed great numbers over a page.
The hair has a wheat scent.
The crow has been flying off into space.
He has gone away now.

Almost from Nowhere

I. Back

She told us to slow down.
Her eyes were luminous and soft.
Her arms were quite strong.
Her body was full of trees
and squash plants, I mean
molecules, you know, charges,
flakes, spinning distant holdings
and infrared glow. Her body was hot
like the nuclear plant, like the springs
back in the foothills, like the glint
at the top of fir trees, or yellow
held open in the hour. Her body was blue,
too, violet, purple, ultrablue and shaded,
and it was feathers of finches and nuthatches,
it was sunflower stalks and heavy heads,
it was brick-walled lunch rooms at break,
it was openings of the wrapped bread
we sit down to, the table steadying
what was wavering, those of us making
what parts of us might be asking,
or ignoring, tuning, the way it might
have been fogged or rained in the afternoon,
the way it might have been steamed up
or felt by folks with extra rings,
the brilliant multicolored gypsy skirts
and slender sandals, the forest nests
secretly coiled and covered by shade
in the slippery and held, by the hand

of sunlit branching. She was true
as warmed-up peppermint leaves
reaching the blood, navying greens
and violet, through evening in her,
and her eyes, her lashes, her . . .

There are many sightings,
the scent of hair, the open look.
There are examples, implyings,
mergings, many that have not gone
within reaches of names, and many
that go back to the mother, or back
to the kiss, back, to breath,
to holding and sway, and cry
and sound, back. Back.

II. Birth Ocean

Heavy kelp forests swaying,
massive waves carrying
the coast, the ocean
a rice being asked, the ocean
an elegant fresh bread of hunger
someone has
brought in
more of,

with each point, sphered
in parallel planes,
blue sky, flaming sky,
ocean rain sky, layered ground
and sky, underground, ground
and sky—until

suddenly the ocean
is everywhere, all atoms
moving in the wave
of its breathing,
its red root nested
in the Vajrayana void
it might be,
breathing up birth
of the world
exactly now
into the wave
that won't stop
and never started,
for which we have
evolving heart.

Say a hunger shattered
a mother stone into a pool
of stones—probably the ocean
was bringing small yellow finches
into the dark-red distance.
And this is the world
we were waiting for.

III. Mother/Matter

As the sound of the rain is shielding.
As someone walks past carrying your tangent
   scent of oranges.
As bark forms for decades on a chestnut trunk,
   the red coals still simmering in the stove,
   and how much of us is still unborn?
Mother grass, mother the broken lake.
Mother on the steel table under the spotlight
   and my body flying a thousand miles away
   in the doctor's hands.
Mother the wild curry, the soft field.
We play the African metal bells, listening
   for your breath in the rain
   lightly reaching our skin.
I see how much I miss
   the trees when we were one.
I remember your kiss on my infant belly
   in the infinity of all else.
Now in the mock-up mirroring wave
   I know you would have me see
   each place is center of this world.
I know the stone is mother stone,
   and I feel part of me still
   to be born, like part of each person,
   part of each animal, and each thing.
Resting, in the evening, our heat falls
   into the falling center
   of the falling world
   you hold and carry close to you.
As the wind in the leaves is your breathing.

IV. Fir Needles

The bridge shakes as the industrial train
passes over open time. Almost from nowhere
a man appears full of love for Van Gogh.
Fir needles drop and more of them form.

The tabla player seems to be floating.
The floor is the shadow of his drumming.
Nearby dancers suddenly are sensuous,
in their whole bodies, light carried by music.

A woman dives after the body and pulls her out
of the cells. Orange squash blossoms unfold
in their self-grown jungles almost overnight.
The mother brings a future like deep memory.

The growl of the Doberman part of God's voice
stops some people. The weeping at the scene
of the emergency burns with a first fire.
Saying anything more might be a mistake.

The people with serious needs are part of us.
The flames of mistakes and ideas to help
are part of us. We are part of them.
Fir needles drop and more of them form.

The mother holds the baby like deepening memory.
Every breath knows it is part of the wind.
The tabla player drums visceral light back out.
Saying anything returns as something needed.

V. The New Young

Carried by the wind,
a new generation has been arriving,
like seeds from a neoclassical dome
exploded at the end of a stalk,
like angry settlers not believing
what senators report.

Carried by the water
in their blood and brains,
they are slowly taking their places
in between the old buildings.

The screens snap on.

**

They will be heard though some are quiet right now.
They will be strong and might go off to a war.
They will tune the strings of the weaving machines
to the way skin likes to be touched by fabric.

They will invent new handicaps and general maxims,
and some houses will be mansions with virtual rooms,
hidden landings, virtual massive parks to go to
after the workday, where sweat will be as real

as ever, where each human eye will have formed
from its first mergings in the first cells
and display by shape and color intelligence
of the species, the astonishing iridescence.

**

These folks are flying in behind the stealth jets.
They are climbing off the heavy backs of horses
or out from beneath the chassis of machines.
Some of them have our faces and some
faces we have never seen before.

And many have already seen farther
than we have imagined.

VI. Union

The words about union threaten some people.
When fir trees become part of our bodies
and sea lions in Newport Bay are wild sisters,

when etchings of beach grass say something
as the wind guides them, people who want control
are thinking of something else, something focused

more, but not of the look of the elephantine rock,
not the sculpted driftwood stumps that swivel
in waves as if the beach were speaking in sign,

not the blue drifting between stratospheric pauses,
or the slow current in the sand as we walk.
And from under the waves, meaning propels us.

Cities of stone and light settle into the hills.
Lost nations return in the quietness of a speaker.
So when the scent of the beach lifts from a city street

and voices of hitchhikers linger by parked cars,
when the squirrel suddenly looks into a living person,
when the nuthatch wakes up and sees what is moving,

when people confuse talk with meaning and people
hear what they were expecting, when a scapegoat
enters the room and some of the dark night lifts,

cities of stone and light settle into the hills.
When the rose breaks open on the side of a jet,
when an octopus hunts in the muddy bottom of crystals,

when a dog guides someone through the late markings,
when stockings on smooth legs become the clock,
when uncles forgive before they try to listen,

when industry parks its bus under a galaxy,
when sparrows repeat the beauty of a father,
lost nations return in the quietness of a speaker.

When ropes tied to a ship were going nowhere,
when workloads scrambled with beetles in the woods,
when women were known for their strength among us,

when much could be thought and much of it was true,
when the ocean could be heard, were we there,
and our fire and our rains and our grasses?

VII. Saturday

Tall firs and cedars
circle the neighborhood.

A few of the crows
shout, having a good time
surviving.

I fly in some of the healing
dreams, and do not believe
I am sleeping,
as if nothing could hurt me.

**

When I hear the crows,
sometimes I wake up more,
grateful to be alive
near their power.

But of course it is so easy
to become bewildered,
with all the work,
with the tens of thousands
of cars and trucks
gunning down the highway,
burning the wealth
of the planet
carefully.

I toss the coins again:
"Under heaven thunder rolls."

And "Care of the cow
brings good fortune."

**

I don't know what I have—
the birds, the firs, my body,
the people in my life,
this place, everything
I can think of?

A nuthatch takes a sunflower seed
and flies to a hazelnut limb
out back.

I love the brown eyes of cows
and the brilliance of blue jays
who are so alive.

In the afternoon
lit by rain or sun,
the scent of blackberry branches
lifts from the ravine.

Overhead, solar systems churn
elegantly, like molecules
in part of an immense body
so unthinkable the living beings
on this planet
are like chance neutrinos
in one of the atoms.

**

Suddenly it is beautiful night.
What we have thought
and applied to things
empties as the night sky
is more and more alive
in the molecules
and open air
of each cell
and synapse,
forever.

Vanilla-Scented Newspaper of Existence

Wrecking balls swing over the word *vanilla*.
Vanilla is released, as they pummel it
into the air people are breathing
in the small town by the frozen river.

It's a spring day by this iced river,
no a winter day, no a spring day,
can't really tell when everyone is inside
by their Multihued Screens of Eternity.

Vanilla enters eternity as a man tries to pray.
One manager who is also a man gets a hernia.
One wrecking ball breaks into encyclopedic
utterances of scholars working at the bank,
which is a construction site
where people are building a tower
to overlook all the planet.

The whole process is taking too long,
and besides the planet is round,
with too much curving off, vanishing
beyond the horizon. This doesn't stop
tellers from listening to their superiors.
It doesn't stop sparrows and finches
from appearing and disappearing
in the face of great cats at the Zoo
of Eternity that the bank is trying
to swallow like a half-dissolved lozenge.

It seems the bank's mouth is always open
and the great cats are hungry far beyond
anything caretakers can put a hand on
when they try to help people in highrises
from speaking before they think.
Everyone speaks before they think,
more than a few had been arguing.

For some reason, the plaza smells
like vanilla mixed with cat markings.

If you've ever had a male cat
spray your pillow, you know
what all this is pointing to.

Of course, if you haven't,
you wouldn't be reading this.
At least, that's what I tell myself
as I read the vanilla-scented Newspaper
of Existence someone abandoned
late at night near my front door.

Snow Falling

And snow was the ground falling
back to its bed.

Beds were how houses formed
around them.

And hair was the way ancients had hair.

Before money was baking in the vaults.
Before penicillin ached in its healing.

        **

In the glow of red coals,
we had faces lit by bison, the heat
of cedar roots, the outside dark
loosening its muffled wave breaking
over and over the day.

And snow was the sky of coals some boy saw
two cities away, that a man on the deck
felt in the crystals
littered in pulsings,

near a girl whose hand was opening
or closing, a mother whose house was luminous
from a seed falling, another woman
whose horse was breathing by a night tree,
perhaps with distant drumming.

There's more, not enough
but still more, like bodies
we walk with our own

in future centuries. Their blood in our bones,
charged, all this paying of attention
in half-sun, with half-moon
reverberating fog energy
this snow is.

And now when someone
notices, the energy is changed.
The energy is changed for the managers
of apricot streetlights, for the drummers
whose rhythms are wise or unwise,

everything bread on the tongue
of that falling snow

with promised equations
and knit gloves
and blue wall that is a wave
of phone calls, it is falling,

fathers of moods, brothers and daughters
of the white sky falling, sisters
and sons of the snow.

II.

As I watch the bright stars shining, I think

a thought of the clef of the universes and of the future.

—Walt Whitman

What Changes Has the Primal
Nighttime Sky

The house-lit rain can fall back to its nests
and silver light it sees with find the air
a sanctuary, for glowing breath, say,
and bones felt sinking underneath the road
make clocks with open arms thrown out to chance,
their undercurrent pressing into thought
some waves that shape us—where old sun might flare
the hot horizon back in flaming skies.
We sense old mammal-caring inside this,
that, carried, will protect totemically
and form its body from our spines and bloods,
with formal holds we hope can hold us here.

From this underground, the rain is steaming
after being rocked in human longing.
The tigered holy months will make us whole,
or silver light will take on violet dusk
when leaves unfold their source into night air.
We sense we might return to ancient sense,
on a night like this, centered with loose hold,
but held by the center of the planet.
We ask, and give by asking burdens back.
We bring to earth what earth will let us have.
And honest reaching has its weight that dreams
roam in, like fossils, like escaped horses.

Preparing for Work

And when the stamp on the postcard from Dan
in Nepal showed a white rhinoceros, alert,
like a locomotive deep in another frequency,

sprawled on a bed, someone
was explaining esoteric psychological nuances,
as a Norway maple presented
only a portion of its maple tonality
and sunrise moralities lifted
a thick mushroom gladly
into the downed ancient firs.

Suddenly, old Saudi Arabian eye shadow
from tax forms was part of the dust
falling on ancient skeletons
that had reassembled,
some 50 feet tall, some still alive,
as part of some psychic block.

A medieval night city of glowing coal
had been seen from the foothills
after dark, as the house where the child lived
with some shame was still around in the body,
as if the night's dream weren't ending.

That is, a woman had been petting
a wild reindeer on his thick spine
as he groaned like a dog.
Behind them were camps
of military tents dusted
by decades of incineration.

When some panther bolted in the library,
we ran through fire doors
like at the factory and tried to stop him
in the steel hallway welded onto the school.

One of the Days

There is so much working into itself, becoming what it was,
   moving on and staying, heavy or lifting with rain.
And so much earth in the ounce of bread, so many holes
   in the light for breathing, so much radio reaching
   a doorway before or after someone we see, so much
   yellow-black grosbeak gone suddenly.
And train cars off to future unthinkable cities,
   brushstrokes of pollen worked up from the shuffled cards,
   so much scent of skin or hair and face lit by a tree.
So much cottonwood, resilient feather's strength,
   gentleness in unnamed place, garden in one of the days.

                    **

This newly born sky of one of the mornings.
Those difficult healings, factories floating
   on their oil, rustlings of sheet
   music over barren loading docks.
It's all right to look past what some do
   and see soul in the body and feel
   soul in the light,
   before anything happens.
Before the century's arguments.

                    **

Like fluorescence
   in a corner office of the factory,
   the mystery comes in whisperings
   impossible to locate, maybe

in hieroglyphs, or the nectarine
bend of a body.
Like an uncle whose mind has filled
with the night sky, the radiant
swell of sourdough, broccoli's
backbone of glowing water,
a kitchen window inside clarity.
But like a daughter who is
of herself, the way water
is in the air that is alive.

Bach, Celery, Elephant Paintings

At what point does radio break through?
Yo-Yo Ma on cello, back in the evening,
   what could be more right for the shift
   of a century than Bach from a previous age?

When judges compare artists, isn't it they ask
   which is better, celery or eggplant, a heron
   or a chickadee, a street or a vapor trail,
   B-flat or C-sharp minor? Does the workweek resound?
What is it like to have an elephant suddenly walking
   quietly in a gymnasium? Has contrabass been dropped?
Have you ever felt yourself standing with elephants
   who one by one lift the bones of the dead
   regardingly into the air for centuries?

Say you have a brother, a desk stacked with books,
   a zoo person collecting abstract paintings
   done by elephants, celery and eggplant,
   the elephants who have been doing the paintings,
   the janitors following everyone around,
   the book throwing off Bach and Bartok shadows,
   what do you have then as best, next best, and so on?

After DeKooning had been sent paintings by an elephant
   and he had written back praising the new talent,
   what was the look on his face
   when he heard who had painted them?
The first person who wrote the word *evolution*,
   what was the look on her face?
Take some of the artistry of apes, sensitivity

of certain dogs, planning of octopi, joy and sorrow
of many birds—what does the cello say then?
Who is it the moon honors?

Sleep Closes Its Rock-Lit Yards

And I wake with my whole body into your arms,
and then into the house, the wooden floors

and chairs flowing in grain, waking
beneath the trees moving with sunlight

and green oceans in each leaf cell following
a swirling starlight over the earth

even through daylight, cottonwoods
towering with cries of the finches,

the dwarf-faced bark luminous and shaded
still, and slender almonds shaded

in their morning shapes on the table
in the green bowl by last evening's papers,

the sparrow's root song working in the flow
of grain, of the last sleep waking

onto the earth, where we learn to see
nothing is more than being here together,

that silence wakes the wooden day
a person waking gives back to his body,

to the faint mushrooms, or the doors.
I step into the living room and feel

the clothing of women and men now far away
woven into our huge circling braided rug,

laced with its years blossoming outside
their formed houses and lives, given back

in the grain, in our room where we wake,
knowing one of us will move into the other's

arms and our breasts will touch, and our faces,
in the weeks and years inside us.

The Scent Where Lightning Hit
Calls Us to Sleep But Then Wake

I.

Sky over the planet
is blue with longing.
There is so much we want,
and so much lost.

Under quantum streetlight
or near the glow of moss,
we want the first birth
of things to be born!

II.

Earth is a feather
the mountain raven left.
We want our lives to live,
and so much in the bearing.

Major atonal chords bend,
struck by string quintets.
I want to keep listening
until the world is round.

III.

Through black bear walking,
our earth root deepening,
wheat of the miles, windy
rains over sea-thunder,

through mind lifting
from certain smallness,
we want so much to live
and this hour to be born!

Between Ground and Space

I. Workweek Drive

Now the iron-wheeled clock gears drive.
The gold-dipped chains spark longingly.
A rose vanishes in a cool spectroscope
politely, as lemon-tongued
ventures plant slow kisses
of industrial steam into the sky.
If only the sky were open enough
or a sparrow's verge could mark
the depth. If only a geyser
could cure, back into the spell,
the old voices fluted, mossed,
coming from solid things
the way those things
came from the ground.

Touched by peppery sea-night
and by the long afternoon's
almond, people meet at work
from back in some of the past.
Nearby, the small burgundy brush
moves through someone's long hair.
A call breaks through the room.

II. Morning

The new bread just out,
scent of espresso, shrill
steam foaming new milk
in the steel pitcher,

her indigo in the reaches,
engines along the edges
of river air,

new moon over the apples
held by their leaves.

III. Between Ground and Space

Darkened indigo night
the Bombay sun left inside us,

the figure of someone we lost
poling a black Italian boat
between wave-lit dark-red bays,

a pitch-black Incan solitude,
ferns glowing from thick shoulders,

this night the sun keeps sliding
between sheets of pungent ground
and endless Galapagos mathematics
out through the opening gaze
of great orbiting telescopes,

as the child asks you a question
just to be more near you now,
from the reaches, a guitar
that stopped but still is heard,
contrabass Tibetan chanters
still heard in ambient sound,

a small hand touching you.

IV. Pumpkins

A few pumpkins ripen
toward the end
of their long vines.

The fiery wheel of decibels,
the blue dome of the daytime
capitol of molecules,
our wild ancestry, faces
seen in passing buses,
the striving waverings
on massive silver counters

sometimes return
to this plant
and its long birth.

V. Squash Blossoms

Science reveals the infrared lure.
The raccoon hangs snug a while
on the hazelnut branch.
The large ferns spread open
further after the watering.

We watch as they teach us their art,
however short our lives are.

Now the orange squash blossoms
open through the gate of sunlight
for thousands of years.

VI. Workday

Our hands with their bones
and nails, dresses
luminous on a Paris avenue,
glass jars holding
parts of old machines,
the overpass shadow
growing a few blankets,

and fruit of the oxygen,
afternoon pollen
riding the core of light,
in the dark-red distance
a small thing brings with it
into the human room.

VII. Sun and Winter Night

The sun blossoms alive
in a spinal disk,
its door hinged to the gold
Greek ghosts, its apples
planted into actual apples,
its center of circling:
molecular, primal.

And ignited by signs on the road,
its night follows the flooding
to make space for the morning,
as it longs, taking away
a little more of the slowness.

And sleeping inside us,
ultraviolet, sun for more
than a full month, guiding us
back in ancient power,
it holds us, the night,
close to home in the winter.

April 1999

Today fog soaks out of the ground
and out of the pavement
over what can't be seen.
And now more can't be seen.
The fog floats up out of the river,
as if something will soon
need to be decided.
                              So who can imagine
ten thousand people driven from their homes,
standing together? What mathematician
can multiply that by forty, or fifty?

The fog steams off the bodies
of slugs and out of the breath
of newly born garden spiders, swirling
around photographs of the ten thousand,
multiplied by ten thousand it could be.

                    **

We eat pretty well—baked halibut last evening,
steamed broccoli, tangerines from Florida.
And then while eating, there was all the bread
anyone could want, right here, all the bread
a person could want.
                              Now photography burns
into the brain around the world
the exiled ten thousand at the end
of a Bosnian railroad lined with bombs,
ten thousand in a single place,
starving, many without gloves,

some without shoes, their birth certificates
flaming in looted government buildings
in towns that they just left.

Fog steams up from the sports page,
the millionaire athletes
guarding one another, the statistics,
hundreds of shots, thousands
in an auditorium.
                              Fog exudes
from the opinion pages and swells
out of the ten thousand paragraphs.
Work goes on. The daffodils hold
steady. What are the trees
talking about? I can barely hear them.
The fog thickens in the fog.

Daffodil

The sun starts it all up.
The daffodil trumpets
and leans down.

I looked out over the city
and saw the sun draining.
I saw silver crosses
hurtling mathematically over massive
buildings of another century
and landing in the cemetery
of conscious rebellion. Air Force jets
and long arc-roofed huts by the runway
were reminding us
of raw power over us all these years
that disc through soil of thinking,
loosening ambient sadness, asking
for existential salvation.

But where can we recover
the real angel's words
that probably sound like intricate
chords, or saxophone duets? Sure,
a horse had been walking right through
the month without question,
with many kinds of infrawoven beating
from animals' chests, with steamships
on the horizon with its planetary curve,
the highway near the river
of sanctuary expelling its cars.

The yellow trumpet flower
glows in the sun-flooded sky's mouth
we stand in, behind
the afternoon house
long after it's gone.

A Few of the Hopes

I. Candling Space

Some days we doubt we deserve
such a chance, such a peace,

given this much room to move,
given this much free form and time,

but then the sun fills fir trees
and ignites from inside sudden thrushes,

from heavy swells in a few guitar jams,
as houses vibrate with a stillness,

as if the ocean moon were a snowplow
and we were falling snow, buried

to again appear, growing longer then
longer into this time, into the waves.

On clear nights here you can see
with your solar plexus the candling sky,

rocking planet, the cradling space.
You can feel it with your moving,

birth of song in a further generation,
all the kelp forests constantly swaying,

so many stones of focusing thought,
thunder of heart, all humble rain.

II. By Grace

A low-slung Oldsmobile sedan swerves and rolls
on back-night streets, through scattered lights.

Remember when the man in charge of anger stood
in front of us, and it was fear that fell in?

It lives such a long time and listens to the news
for bombs going off or climbers lost now, close by.

The yogi sits in front of the fear and contemplates
its independence. Shark-skinned consultants shake it.

Carnival rides circle—maybe the fear can be scared off.
Maybe it can be painted by Münch or Dali out of us.

Music thunders on the fast roads. Out ahead somewhere,
21st century war ignites, with huge pre-Christian gongs.

I pull back into my shell, this body and time,
and look around the room, amazed at what is here.

III. Meadowlark in Colorado

Can you still see Langland's horses
breaking loose, galloping up a fog
of reddened dust, turning at the bluffs
back into a canyon where animals
forgive people, where they suddenly
stand, heads down, beneath ancient
cottonwoods no one but them can find?

The galloping of the workweek doesn't have this
elegance. Derricks bend over a field
of direct sadness, cranking and pumping
their grasshopper legs that fell out
of a hawk's beak, the clock arm turning
them around over and over, the oil
washing their wind pipes, the ground
beneath them slowly hollowed out.

A meadowlark can break the spell of gears.
Its trill, open-throated—so much
certainty coming from such a small
brother. The yucca stalks are alert,
motionless, over the miles revealing
what must be joy sunlight carries
sometimes holding the distance together,
releasing it and holding it.

From the tops of yucca and poles
along the road, the song breaks
not far from where we live
with what must be joy, some of the trills
as if wood were intricately carved,
some of the red rock with faces showing
through, bison flanks, abstract
art in some of the red sound,
as this bird maintains
and finds elevation.

May animals
watch over us.

IV. In Circling

The afternoon builds, it waxes,
it sings as a sparrow, it slams
the hood at the station, it sends
and receives, its milk is delivered,
and it wanes, it becomes night.

Then night, mountain canyon night,
its factories cooling, the newspapers
lighting up like match flames, night
waxes, it smoothly explodes
with ultraviolets, it seals the envelope
of wishes, it drops out of hand. It sweeps
with its nervous searchlight, its thudding
car stereos, its asking that opens and closes.
It slides and cranks, it wanes, thins, becoming
morning, cleared away, and afternoon.

So the afternoon builds, waxes,
and night falls, thins, becoming then
the morning, lengthening, afternoon.
A person at work can remember, from inside
this slow identity of flowing, the shaded rush
from which the next world emerges,
drives and wanes, becoming the rest
it finds, becoming sleep.

The vision of countless numbers
around this one place, waxing, to wane,
becoming the next that opens,
breathes, its core ignited, now.

May some of the nearby planet
keep this circling clear.

V. *This Goes On*

The sun brings it up.
The wooden floor holds.

And what has taken so long
suddenly does not move.

Kandinsky fields impressions
rushing out through time.

In the Rauschenberg, red
Vietnam is present tense,

and W.W.II is present tense.
When we met last week,

it's still present suddenly,
and when the trumpet stopped.

The shout and apology sit
breathing, side by side,

on a bench in the locker room
of those sorts of things.

The baby someone holds is someone
holding the baby. Yesterday,

that lunch, the tuna fish
present on the table, the milk

squirting into the calf's mouth,
the look on her face before

and after, all there, shaped,
non-biodegradable, stacking up

in the room, heaped at the edge
of the city, floating upside down

in the river—jugs of it, flapping
sheets in the wind of it here.

Wait, the traffic is creeping
along, faster, things are loosening.

The backs of the heads now
are leaving in waves, passing,

and even the books are flaking,
crumbling, banks of the river

sludding in, paintings yellowing,
darkening, centuries passing,

part of new languages taking over
and further pinpoint technologies.

It's all rushing past. I'll say
so long now. With everything

flooding past, it's already been
said and it's going, it's gone.

Willie Mays, Ted Williams,
Bob Dylan, Adrienne Rich,

Monty Python, Grandma Moses,
all the firemen, the dancers,

all the spark plugs, tables,
Oscars, the three-penny nails,

the blue glass with sunlight
showing through, the thick moss

out back, flying into past tense,
passing now like beach thunder,

like boos at the wrestling arena,
massive rumbling trains of dark

arenas shuddering past,
trenches of horses galloping

up a river, crows dissolving
at the edge of brightening

in the east: the morning present
now, holding the trees, passing

down the streets, waking weight
and time into present tense,

the single bus, the sporty cap,
the dog, the two dogs, the face,

the part of the song, just us
walking here in the present,

the museum opening, the Rothko
shuddering still, taking so long.

Ocean Thunder

On one of the cold nights,
we drove to the Pacific Coast.
A block away from the beach,
we could hear waves booming and rolling.

Up close, the thunder
of those Pacific waves was like what?—

hearing mountains
inside the space that forms them,

the crests at the top of their sound
riding their inside miles?

Each sound was followed by quiet rolling
as the wave surged back
away from anything solid,
withdrawing under contrabass wholeness,

beneath light that is living,
back into ocean thickness that is living.

**

The weight of the ocean
thunders steadily, like freight trains
that don't stop passing by a small town.

The weight of wild starlight
that waves carry ignites the sound

of the dark water. Dreams are nearby,
under the waves, whales migrating down from Alaska
if it's late fall, wind shaking the house with its water,

the rains coming in one after another
from their months at sea,

the rains with their Baltic darknesses,
their Laotian drift and Himalayan violet-gray lulls.

Some of the water has housed Pacific dolphins,
Hawaiian humpbacks, middle-of-the-sea turtles,
and fluorescent jellyfish
within months
of its sliding layers.

Where the surface layer is breaking,
full sound roars from space
of the ocean,
into the rain.

Huge Choir Roar

Now everyone is singing at once,
   everyone thinking at once.
Every woman or man from a rushing car.
Every car engine burning the gasoline of sound.
Every factory machine stamping oiled thunder.
Every person looking at a stained glass
   window with mouth open.
Everyone holding a pencil, everyone
   touching a key, everyone in an office
   of state, everyone in a store.
Everyone is singing at once
   after the single grievings.
Everyone is here at the border
   of what can be heard.
Everyone on stage is singing
   open-throated, open-vowelled,
   holding a long question all at once,
   then they stop.

Only the piano, some strings, basses.

Then everyone is singing at once.
Every person sitting at a table.
Every boy tying a shoe, every girl
   mashing potato, every work glove,
   every tin of tobacco, every clock
   is going off at once.
Everyone who can get out of bed
   is singing, intoning, great chord
   not quite a chord as an ocean sound,

a human ocean sound, a sun
of a sound, not joyful only
or sad, but present, now!
Singing, all at once—
then it stops.

(listening to Arvo Pärt)

Rhododendron Pollen

Rhododendron pollen
showers the neighborhood.

Pollen swirls in the ant's face.

As ancestors glow from cells,
are we to worry about integrity of eggshells,
to consider lost letters of the alphabet,

to not leave the body in order to know what this is?

When everything became ocean and was itself.

When avenues were working through breathing
of plants and also stones that breathe
solid with the air, solid in breath,
solid until end.

**

Pollen gusts, sun falling, young cliffs,
the golden mean, paintings of human regard,
cooking tar and road dust, grasshoppers
and gull screes, rows of blank or lively
houses, wind making a blanket over fear,
my father dying, the look in his eyes
when he couldn't move, the silence

when a physician asked him the day
of the week, the night showing a fragment
of 125 billion galaxies moving through
openness their moving makes,
person in the body, the slow bass
chord beneath what is known,

a sparrow wildly singing from the roof,
the bass chanting becoming what a soprano
reaches, aligned, relative to a particular hand,
leaves forming where there weren't any,
the planet circling the way it calls things back,
the way the core of it is a sun.

**

Air fired by what it might do,
skin that drinks from promise
exhaling freely, a sky of years
passing in a shoe sound, a taste
of bread, a blue jay flash, a crooked twinge,
an ant under a rhododendron looking up
as pollen showers his looking,
where the work of union breaks
into many, and body flies into the sun.

This evening flies through its opening,
the feathers of its body
through next knowing,
where what we gave
was what we had.

Marigolds Out Back

The tidal wave of rhododendron pollen.

Motor cars of the night universe.

Marigolds in the garden breathing
as we breathe, only backwards, inside out,
singing without sound we can hear, rowing
last year's graves into the mid-air valley
of raw sunlight...

Marigolds holding
spiraled DNA out in their petals.

Fir trees holding marigolds up by parallelism.

If the oars are lost,
let the fir trees row—
they're already doing it.

      **

Grasses and bushes sway and shake
as our hair moves slightly.

Does the water know what it's doing?
Does the starlight filter
heaviness of all vacuum?

Do the owls fly when we don't see them?

Pray for the grail of the ocean's emptiness.

How many children
make up a person?

Hold the blue name in the blue sky.

Hieroglyphics on the No-Wall

"Without the energy of the shutter which bangs on the no-house."

—*K. Patchen*

The words she gave
keep reshaping.
They are still alive,
until—what is it?—
until the sparrows in them
don't show up?

*I fell asleep one
time,* someone says,
*but then when I endeavored
to wake, I saw
I wasn't completely
successful. So I went
to work. That's what I do.*

His hand in his pocket,
money in his fingers,
a man hears talk of a new war
dying back down. Boys
with their heads buzzed clean
smoke by the encaged grocery
and almost do not speak. A woman
in a dark brown business suit
steps, her heels clicking,
lifting her taller, and taller,
into the architect's office.
The day sloshes in the back
of the van the painters are using.
A man with almost nothing on
runs past and vanishes.

Jellyfish parachuting
through the ocean,
ancient reborn grandfathers,
blood in the black letters
of newsprint blending
invisibly, rapids
of calmest rivers,
one guy turning a key
in a skeleton, one gal
in a darkest day still
lit by sun, the yellow-green
apple glowing in the bin
of yellow-green apples—
suddenly nothing is sacred.
Then all things are sacred.
The simple instructions
have complications.
The overhead lights
have sun in them.
The cellos work
all night for months
making their ocean's
land, in living cells, rain
falling onto the ground.

A Lincoln sedan swerves.
Behind the wheel an ancestral senator
makes his face like a professional
photograph of himself in the collective.
Behind his face is an unclear teen.
Suddenly the sedan bursts into flames
of a campfire, on the Pacific beach,
under a billion lights in the sky
and only a few of them seen.

Music thunders on the fast roads
and pumps, criss-crossing city sky.
If a bomb went off, it might be radio,
the whole hour in ultramagnetic bands,
the night wind where lit flames swim.
Let them pass, let them pass,
let them pass right through us,
someone sings. Let it pass,
let this pass, let them pass
right through us, someone sings.
And the more that someone sings,
the more another shuts the open
door as sky grinds its teeth
in the mouths of animals

move, ⟶

slowly in underground caves
where disappointment let loose
shadows of the species.

One after the other, in replays
replays, all merging in the

cars plow up night
with their mercury
headlights needling
the skin of undersleep.
It could be the sparrow
in the cedar by the house,
the silence
in her whispering.

It could be Dali's realism
that is so surrealistic,
or Klee's child marks
in the margins adults find
arresting, or moonlight
with a face, or the rich
fog souping up. *I'm nobody,*
really, you know, says someone
walking, the fog pulling
the evening where it has taken
the other evenings.

Energy to you through storms and thunders
Of the slow merge, energy of iridescent steel-blue
Wind flying out of the sun, children with so much longing,
Set-backs hammered into chords riding the transcordant plow,
Birth wind asking, *What is it we came here to do?*

Auspicious Starlight

We'd come far,
as half-moon rose
between branches aspens held above
what we know. We had reached

the crystal call of nuthatches,
web-splitting winds
retiring mistakes,

orange-scented rooms
of an inner house, the outer space
labs wheeling over troubles,
as if eleven Tibetan lamas
had conjured speeds we need

to heal
what has been wounded
in the Orphic wail.

We had walked what we love
not far from furnaces
of intense success
people near us built against sheer loss.

** **

The paper we were written on
was light reaching the planet.

Working, resting,
all returned to soul.

When breaking open syntax,
we heard what held us down
to grounding: central sun
that drew these atoms
into living light.

What happened when we could not be ourselves
hounded the people
we had worked to be,
the way a call dies back into gardens,

future children sleeping in gusts,
nothing having been here before
in 2001 of time expanding
its turquoise and yttrium,
its electroosmotic evening fog
by new apples, gingers
that root back by birthing,

after Pacific nighttime sky
ignited a few ancient signs
that found us here
in vast silence.

Acknowledgments

American Writing: "Back"

Barnabe Mountain Review: "Three from the Oregon Coast," "Hieroglyphics on the No-Wall"

The Bitter Oleander: "Daffodil," "Workweek Drive," "Morning," "Between Ground and Space," "Pumpkins," "Squash Blossoms," "Sun and Winter Night," "In Circling"

Black Moon: "Pumpkins"

Calapooya Collage: "Union"

Fine Madness: "Candling Space," "By Grace," "Meadowlark in Colorado," "This Goes On"

Firebush: "This Light, This Lightning," "Ocean Thunder," "Auspicious Night"

The Heartlands Today: "Walking as the Air Cools Slightly"

Heliotrope: "Bach, Celery, Elephant Paintings," "Huge Choir Roar"

Manzanita Quarterly: "What Changes Has the Primal Nighttime Sky"

Northeast: "Sleep Closes Its Rock-Lit Yards"

Pemmican: "Was It Like Drinking Water Out of the Rain," "Under the Sun"

Poetry Northwest: "The New Young"

The Raw Seed Review: "One of the Days"

Rhino: "Snow Falling"

South Dakota Review: "The Scent Where Lightning Hit Calls Us to Sleep But Then to Wake"

Talking River Review: "Fir Needles"

The Temple: "Saturday"

Water & Plastic (an anthology): "This Goes On"

Willow Springs: "Birth Ocean," "Hieroglyphics from Wind and the Inside of Seeds," "Marigolds Out Back," "The Night Sky"

Writer's Forum: "Some Adult Theater"

Additionally:

"One of These Days," was included in *Lame Duck Eternity* (26 Books, Portland, OR), 1998.